ACCOUNTANCY

PART-5

:: Author ::

ROBIN N. VORA

(M.COM., B.ED., SLET)
GUJARAT UNIVERSITY RANKER

PUBLISHED BY

The New Era International Publishing House
HQ. At & Po. Chaveli., Ta- Chansma,
Dist- Patan, North Gujarat, India, Asia.

All rights reserved. Any person who does any unauthorized act in relation to this publication may be liable to criminal prosecution and civil claims for damages.

First Publication: 10th FEBRUARY, 2015

Copyright: Author
(c) ROBIN N. VORA

ISBN:- 978-15-08472-73-5

Price: Rs.750/- INDIA
$ 15 OUTSIDE INDIA

PUBLISHED BY

**The New Era International Publishing House
HQ. At & Po. Chaveli., Ta- Chansma,
Dist- Patan, North Gujarat, India, Asia.**

Dedicated to my Parents

INDEX

	Chapters	
1	"Bank Reconciliation Statement"	1
2	"Depreciation Accounting"	16
3	"Reserve and Contingences"	29
4	"Non-Trading Concerns"	42
5	"Accounting Ratio"	68

CHAPTER -1

" Bank Reconciliation Statement "

☐ THEORY SECTION ☐

❖ *Introduction :*

➤ *After deduction of reasons, a statement prepares to reconcile the balance as per bank account and as per passbook, is known as bank reconciliation statement or bank reconciliation.*

➤ *Bank Reconciliation Statement is not an account but it is only a statement it is used in reconciling the balance as per passbook and balance as per bank account after finding out the causes and explaining such differences.*

   *Two things are very important for preparing bank reconciliation statement bank account **in the** books of a trader **i.**e. cashbook and trader's account in the books of a bank i.e. passbook.*

❖ ***Passbook :*** *" Passbook means a copy or extract of a trader's account in the books of a bank ".*

Date	Particulars	Amount withdrawn (debit) Rs	Amount deposited (Credit) Rs	Balance Rs	Signature of a bank officer

❖ **Bank balance and bank overdraft :**

" Debit balance as per either cashbook or bank account is a bank balance.

Credit balance as per either cashbook or bank account is a bank overdraft."

❖ **Bank Reconciliation Statement** :   " Bank reconciliation statement means a statement showing the   causes of difference in the balance of a bank as per cashbook, and a balance as per cashbook, for a particular time or on a particular date ".

Bank reconciliation statement is prepared by a trader for a certain time or on a date because of which the difference between balance of a bank as per cashbook and balance as per passbook can be found out and its causes can be noticed.

❖   **Purposes   or   preparation   and   utility   of   Bank Reconciliation Statement:**

1) *With the help of bank reconciliation statement, reasons of difference, between bank balance as per cashbook and bank balance as per passbook, can be found out.*

2) *As the causes of difference can be found out between both balances, errors committed, if any can be rectified with the help of necessary accounting entries.*

3) *If any transactions is omitted to be recorded in cashbook, information regarding it can be collected and by recording it, correct bank balance can be arrived at.*

4) *If any errors are committed in recording any transactions, they come to know immediately and errors can be rectified e.g a cheque of Rs. 3000 is received but by mistake it is recorded as only rs 300 in bank column of the cashbook.*

5) *By repairing bank reconciliation statement actual bank balance can be known, which is shown in the balance sheet and thereby real economic picture of a business is obtained.*

6) *Embezzlement of cash from bank transactions can be traced out by preparing bank reconciliation statement.*

7) *Compensating errors can be traced out by preparing reconciliation statement. Even when both the balances are the same, it doesn't mean that there Is no reason of difference or error. In that case also, reason of difference or error may be there but they compensate against each other.*

8) By preparing bank reconciliation statement, information can be obtained regarding cheques deposited but dishournured as well as interest, commission, charges etc. recorded by the bank in our account.

❖ ***Reasons for difference in the bank balance as per cashbook and as per Passbook.***

✓ Cheque deposited in bank but not credited by bank : In BRS (Credit/Less)

✓ Cheque issued but not presented for payment : In BRS (Debit/Add)

✓ Direct deposits by customers in bank : In BRS (Debit/Add)

✓ Amount recovered on behalf of a trader and credited to his account by bank but not recorded in cashbook : In BRS (Debit/Add)

✓ Cheque recorded in cashbook but left undeposited in bank : In BRS (Credit/Less)

✓ Cheque deposited in the bank but not recorded in the cashbook : In BRS (Debit/Add)

✓ Cheque issued and presented for payment in a bank account left unrecorded in cashbook : In BRS (Credit/Less)

✓ Cheque recorded in cashbook but not given to traders : In BRS (Debit/Add)

✓ Any amount collected by bank but not recorded in the cashbook : In BRS (Debit/Add)

✓ *Any amount debited by bank but not recorded in the cashbook : In BRS (Credit/Less)*

✓ *Payment made by bank but not recorded in cashbook : In BRS (Credit/Less)*

✓ *Dishonor unrecorded in cashbook of a bill of exchange discounted with a bank: In BRS (Credit/Less)*

✓ *Total of payment side is overcast of a cashbook : In BRS (Debit/Add)*

✓ *Total of payment side is under cast of a cashbook : In BRS (Credit/Less)*

✓ *Total of receipt side is overcast of a cashbook : In BRS (Credit/Less)*

✓ *Total of receipt side is under cast of a cashbook : In BRS (Debit/Add)*

Note :

1) If debit/credit method and balance as per passbook is given then same method we have to apply.

2) If add / less method and balance as per passbook is given then reverse method we have to apply.

❖ **Methods to prepare a bank reconciliation statement**

There are two main methods of preparation of bank reconciliation statement

1) Mathematical method or add-less method

2) Accounting method or debit-credit column method

1) Mathematical method or add-less Method :

When add-less method i.e. mathematical method is used for the preparation of bank reconciliation statement, it starts with bank balance either as per cashbook or passbook.

Bank reconciliation statement of Shri…….
As on……….

Sr no.	Particulars	Amount withdrawn Rs
	Bank overdraft as per cashbook	5,000

Debit balance of a bank account as per cashbook means a bank balance, and credit balance of a bank account as per cashbook means bank overdraft. Debit balance of a bank account as per passbook means bank overdraft and credit balance of a bank account as per passbook means a bank balance.

This rule is under. " Do what other have done".

2) Debit-credit method of accounting method :

as per this method of preparation of bank reconciliation statement amount column is classified into two parts viz. debit and credit here, as per cashbook if there is a debit balance of a bank (bank balance), it is *recorded in debit column and if there is a credit balance (i.e. bank overdraft) it is recorded in credit column similarly as per passbook, if there is a credit balance of a bank (i.e. bank balance overdraft) it is recorded in debit column.*

☐ PRACTICAL SECTION ☐

*1. On 28-2-03 bank balance as per passbook of **Krishna** is **Rs.10,000** which does not agree with the bank balance as per cashbook. From the following information prepare a bank reconciliation statement of Krishna.*

*(1) Cheque of **Rs. 10,000** were deposited in bank but out of these, cheques of **Rs.4,000** only were credited by bank upto **28-2-03**.*

*(2) A cheque of **Rs.4,000** is drawn and recorded in the cashbook but by mistake it was not handed over to a creditor. This cheque is found out from the drawer of a table.*

*(3) Insurance premium of **Rs.12,000** paid by bank is unrecorded in cashbook.*

*(4) A Customer has directly deposited **Rs.20,000** in the bank account. This information was received by Krishna on **1-3-03**.*

*(5) Bank charges of **Rs.100** recorded by the bank, are recorded twice in the cashbook.*

(6) A cheque of **Rs.4,000** which was deposited in bank on 27-2-03 is dishonored. This information was received on 3-3-03.

(7) Cheques of **Rs. 6,000** were issued, out of these cheques of **Rs.4,000** only were presented for payment before 28-2-03.

(8) A cheque of **Rs.4,000** deposited in bank is left unrecorded in cash book and the same is not credited by bank in passbook till today.

(9) In passbook bank has credited **Rs.200** for bank interest and debited **Rs.120** for bank charges.

(10) Total of the receipt side of the cashbook is overcast by **Rs.4,000**.

2. **From the following information prepare a bank reconciliation statement of Reema.**

Dr   *Cash Book (Bank Account)*   Cr

Date	Receipt	Rs.	Date	Payments	Rs.
2003 April 1	To balance c/d	1700	2003 April 3	By Pintoo's A/c	1250
2	To Meet's A/c	1500	5	By devershi's A/c	250
4	To Mihir's A/c	1000	6	By salary a/c ((a cheque given to Umangi)	500
8	To Monkia's A/c	2500	7	By Insu. Prem. A/c (A cheque given to LIC)	1500

9	To Aesha's A/c	3000	10	By Minakshi's A/c	2000
22	To Kiran's A/c	3500	18	By Krina's A/c	1500
			24	By Seeta's A/c	500
			28	By Priynka's A/c	4500
			30	By Usha's A/c	500
			30	By balance C/f	700
		13,200			13,200

Pass Book

Date	Particulars	Debit	Credit	balance
2003 1	Balance c/d		1700	1700
April2	Meet's A/c		1500	3200
3	Pintoo's A/c	1250		1950
4	Mihir's A/c		1000	2950
7	LIC's A/c	1500		550
10	Minakshi's A/c	2000		2050
18	Krina's A/c	1500		2050
22	Kiran's A/c		3500	1450
28	Prinka's A/c	4500		3050
30	Bank interest A/c		50	3000
30	Usha's A/c		500	2500
30	Balance c/f		2500	2500
		10750	10750	
2003 May 1	Balance c/d	2500		2500

3. *From the following information prepare a bank reconciliation statement of Shri Ritu for the month of Nov,2003.*

Dr   **Cash Book (bank Column)**   **Cr**

Date	Receipt	Rs.	Date	Payments	Rs.
2003			2003	By bank charges	
Nov.1	To balance c/d	9750	Nov.1	A/c	90
1	To bank interest	150	2	By Palav's A/c	3000
4	To Mercedes A/c	9000	3	By Dhara's A/c	2250
5	To Audis A/c	9000	6	By Salary A/c (To Veena)	2400
14	To J. K A/c	9000	11	By stationery A/c (to bitu)	6000
16	To Dividend A/c	4500	13	By Akshara's A/c	12000
22	To interest A/c	3000	15	By Mohit's A/c	9600
27	To Varsha's A/c	1500	28	By Rashmi's A/c	2400
			29	By Dipti's A/c	2400
			30	By Trupti's A/c	600
			30	By balance c/f	5160
		45,900			45,900
2003					
Dec 1	To balance c/d	5160			

Pass Book

Date	Particulars	Debit	Credit	balance
2003				
1	Balance c/d		9810	9810
April				
2	Palav's A/c	3000		6810
5	Audi's A/c		9000	15,810
6	Veena's A/c	2400		13,410
13	Akashara's A/c	12000		1410
16	Dividend A/c		4500	5910
22	interest A/c		3000	8910
29	Dipti's A/c	2400		6510
30	Bank commission A/c	300		6210
30	Insurance premium A/c	15000		8790
30	Maulik's A/c		18000	9210
30	Balance c/f	9210		
2003				
May 1	Balance c/d	44310	44310	

4. From the following bankbook and passbook of **Shri Ekta,** prepare a bank reconciliation statement for the account with bank of Baroda.

Dr   **Bank Book**   **Cr**

Date	Receipts	BOB	SBI	Date	Payment	BOB	SBI
2003				**2003**			
May				**May**			
1	To balance c/d	1250		**1**	By balance c/d		4000

6	To Kirti's A/c	1500		2	By Paresh's A/c	500	
14	To Ashok's A/c	1000	500	3	By Parth's A/c	500	
17	To Anajana's A/c	500	1000	8	By Mihir's A/c		2500
24	To Mayuri's A/c	50	1575	15	By Minal's A/c		500
27	To Hetal's A/c	3000		18	By Meet's A/c	600	400
29	To Dhruvi's A/c		2000	23	By Sidharth's A/c	250	350
31	To dividend A/c	500		25	Salary A/c (to Anuj)	500	1000
31	Balance c/f		4175	31	To commission A/c (to Vaibhavi)		500
				31	By balance c/f	5450	
		7800	9250			7800	9250

Pass Book (BOB)

Date	Particulars	Debit	Credit	balance
2003 May 1	Balance c/d	-	1250	1250
2	Paresh's A/c	500	-	750
6	Kirti's A/c	-	1500	2250
8	Mihir's A/c	2500	-	250
14	Ashok's a/c	-	1000	750
18	Meet's A/c	600	-	150
25	Anuj's A/c	500	-	350
29	Dhruvi's A/c	-	2000	1650
30	Dividend A/c	-	500	2150
31	Bank interest a/c	-	50	2200

31	Bank charges a/c	25	-	2175
31	Bank c/f	2175	-	2175
		6300	6300	
2003 June				
1	Balance c/d		2175	

5. **On 31-7-03** cashbook of **Madhvi** shows a bankoverdraft of **Rs.12,000** which differs from the balance shown as per passbook. From the following information prepare a bank reconciliation statement of Madhvi and also find **2003.**

July 1 cheques of **Rs.14,000** are deposited in bank but not credited by bank.

2 cheques of **Rs.6,000** are issued but not presented for payment in bank.

3 cheques of **Rs. 8,000**are deposited in and credited by bank, but left inrecorded in cqashbook.

4 cheques of **Rs.3,000** are issued and recorded by bank, but left unrecorded in cashbook.

8 bank overdrafr interest of **Rs.150** which is deboted by bank is not recorded in cashbook.

14 A cheque of **Rs.400** which was given to Mansi i.e. recorded in cash book, through oversight as **Rs.4,000.**

19 A bill of exchange of **Rs. 4,000** which was discounted with the bank is dishonored. Bank has recorded the amount with nothing charges of **Rs. 40** No record is made for this *dishonor in cashbook.*

*24 Total of receipt side of a cashbook is overcast by **Rs. 1200.***

*28 Bank has paid for **Rs. 5,000** insurance premium on behalf of Kamya.*

*31 Bank has collected **Rs. 1200** for dividend on behalf of Kamya.*

*31 A cheque of **Rs. 12,000** was given to Roshni, but still the same is not presented for payment.*

*31 A cheque of **Rs.8,000** was received from Ankit and the same was deposited in bank, but till today the same has not been recorded in passbook.*

6. ***Gopal trader*** *has two types of accounts in Bank of Baroda one is a saving account and the other is a current account. From the following information prepare a bank reconciliation statement of Gopal traders for saving account. Bank balance as per passbook is **Rs. 48,000.***

1) *A cheque of **Rs.20,000** is deposited in savings a/c but in cashbook through oversight it is recorded in current account.*

2) *A cheque of **Rs.10,000** is issued to Vaidehi from savings a/c, but still it is not presented for payment.*

3) *Cash of **Rs.8,000** deposited in cuurent account, is left unrecorded in cashbook.*

4) *Cheques of **Rs.20,000** were issued from savings account. Out of these cheques of **Rs. 4,000** are aleready presented*

for payment in the bank and no informations are received for the remaining.

5) *A cutomer has directly deposited **Rs.12,000** and **Rs.28,000** respectively in current account and savings account of Gopal traders.*

6) *Bank has credited and debited interest of **Rs.400** and **Rs.720** in savings a/c and current a/c respectively.*

7) *A cheque of **Rs.5,600** which was issued from savings a/c is paid from current a/c by bank.*

8) *A cheque of **Rs.24,000** is deposited in bank account but still it is not credited in bank passbook.*

............××××××××.........

CHAPTER –2

(*"DEPRECIATION ACCOUNTING"*)

☐ THEORY SECTION ☐

☆ *Meaning*

"Depreciation means a gradual and permanent reduction in the value of an asset due to any reason." Depreciation is an amount written off every year from the cost price of an asset during its useful life.

☆ *Characteristics of Depreciation :-*

➢ *Depreciation is depreciable on the fixed assets of a business. So such assets are also known as depreciable assets. The current or liquid assets (Expect loose tools) of a business are not depreciable ex:- stock, cash etc.*

➢ *Depreciation shows a gradual reduction in the usefulness of an asset, by way of the depreciated amount.*

➢ *Depreciation is an expense associated with time.*

➢ *The reduction in the useful value of an asset is gradual and permanent.*

➢ *Depreciation is revenue expenditure. It is debited to P & L a/c in the final a/c.*

➢ *Thought revenue expenditure, depreciation is not payable in cash like salary or rent. Hence, the amount written off as depreciation during a year remains in the business.*

➢ *Depreciation depends not only on time but also on the use of an asset.*

➢ *Normally, the amount of depreciation is written off from the value of a fixed asset at the end accounting year.*

☆ ***Necessity (Objectives) of provision for Depreciation.***

✓ *To consider as a paid Business expenses.*

✓ *To know the true and fair P & L.*

✓ *To know the true and fair financial position of the Business.*

✓ *To Preserve the Capital.*

✓ *To determine the True Cost.*

✓ *To determine the correct selling price of a product or service.*

✓ *To Comply with the Legal Provisions.*

☆ ***Factors Affecting Depreciation (Causes)***

• *Use of an asset.*

• *Passage of Time.*

• *Exhaustion of Quantity.*

• *Permanent Reduction in the Market Price.*

• *Accident.*

- *New inventions and Research.*
- *Natural Factors.*

☆ **Points Affecting the Amount of Depreciation and the Rate of Depreciation.**

  ✖ *Cost price of an Asset.*
  ✖ *Life of an Asset.*
  ✖ *Scrap Value of an Asset.*
  ✖ *Usage of an Asset.*
  ✖ *Repairs And Maintenance Exp.*
  ✖ *Interest on Capital Employed in an Asset.*
  ✖ *New inventions and Research.*
  ✖ *Other Factors.*

☆ **Different Methods of calculating Depreciation:-**

  ❖ *Fixed Installment or Straight Line Method.*
  ❖ *Reducing Balance Method or Written Down Value Method.*
  ❖ *Annuity Method*
  ❖ *Depreciation Fund Or Sinking Fund Method.*
  ❖ *Insurance Policy Method.*
  ❖ *Revaluation Method.*
  ❖ *Compound Interest Method*
  ❖ *Depletion Method*
  ❖ *Mileage Method*
  ❖ *Machine Hour Rate Method.*

✩ *Explanation of Different Method of Depreciation:-*

⇒ *Fixed Installment Method.(Straight Line Method.)*

$$\text{Formula}: D = \frac{c-s}{100}$$

D= Amount of annual Depreciation
C= Cost Price
S= Scrap Value
N=Estimated useful life in years

Note : *When rate of Depreciation is given use the following formula as:*

$$D = \frac{c \times r}{100}$$

D=Amount of annual Depreciation
C= Cost Price
r= Rate of Depreciation

♣ *Advantages :*

1) *This method is very easy from the viewpoint of calculation.*
2) *This method is very simple to understand.*
3) *Every year the same amount of depreciation is written off on as asset.*
4) *This method includes the scrap value of the asset.*

5) *It is assumed that at the end of the useful life of an asset, the balance in the asset account would be equal to or around the estimated scrap value.(zero or estimated scrap value.)*

♣ *Limitations :*

1) *Under this method, the amount of depreciation is the same every year. However, as the asset becomes old, the repairs expenses go on increasing but the amount of depreciation remains fixed. Hence, a balance between the amount of depreciation and the repairs expenses is not maintained.*

2) *The usage of the asset has a greater effect on the depreciation that the passage of time. This point is not considered in this method. However, if an asset is used in more than one shift, then more depreciation should be provided depending on the shifts.*

3) *In future, when the old asset is to be replaced by a new asset, this method fails to make sufficient financial arrangement.*

4) *Capital equal to the cost price of an asset is employed in the asset. This method does not have any provision for interest on this capital.*

♣ *Suitable for which Assets :*

This method is suitable for assets which have a definite useful life e.g patents, trademarks, leasehold assets, etc.

⇒ *Reducing Balance Method (Written Down Value Method)*

$$D = \frac{c \times r}{100}$$

Advantages:-

1) Under this method a balance is maintained between the amount of depreciation and the repairs expenses. In the initial years, more depreciation is charged and thereafter every year the amount of depreciation goes on reducing. On the other hand, repairs expenses are Zero or very less in the initial years and then naturally go on increasing as years pass.

2) It is an easy method to calculate deprecation.

3) Under this method, the value of an asset does not become Zero, during or at the end of its useful life, but is expected to be close to the estimated scrap value.

4) As the income Tax act recognizes this method, it has accepted widely.

♣ Limitations:-

1) This method is complicated as compared to the fixed installment method.

2) This method does not have any provision for interest on capital employed in the asset.

3) At the time of replacement of the asset, the finical provision made by this method is insufficient.

♣ **Suitable for which Assets:-**This method is suitable for assets which have a long useful life ex:- machinery, furniture, fixtures etc.

☆ *Journal Entries For the First year of Purchase of the Asset*

Date	Particulars	L.F	Debit Rs.	Credit Rs.

1	Entry for purchase asset
	Asset a/c Dr.
	    To Bank a/c(purchase price)
	    To Cash a/c(Expenses price)			

2	Entry for Depreciation at the end of the accounting year Depreciation A/c Dr. To Asset A/c			
3	Entry To transfer Depreciation to P & L Account P & L A/c Dr. To Depreciation A/c			

☆ *Difference Between Straight Line Method and Reducing Method.*

No.	Points of Diff.	Straight Line Method	Reducing Balance Method
1.	**Calculation of the amount of depreciation**	*Under this method, the amount of depreciation is obtained by dividing cost price of an asset less its scrap value by the numbers years of estimated useful life, or is determined at the stipulated rate of depreciation.*	*Under this method, the amount of depreciation is determined at the stipulated rate of depreciation for the first year is calculated on the cost price of year it is calculated on the cost price of the asset and thereafter every year it is calculated on the opening balance of the asset of that year.*
2.	**Amount of depreciation**	*As the amount of depreciation at the end of the accounting year is calculated on the cost price of the asset, the amount of annual depreciation is equal every year.*	*As the amount of depreciation at the end of the accounting year is calculated on the cost price of the asset for the first year and thereafter on the opening balance of the asset of the*

			respective year, the amount of annual depreciation goes on reducing every year.
3.	**Amount of depreciation and repairs expenses**	A proper balance cannot be maintained between the amount of depreciation on the asset and its repairs expenses.	A proper balance can be maintained between the amount of depreciation on the asset and its repairs expenses.
4.	**Scrap value of the asset at the end of its useful life.**	The value of the asset at the end of its useful life becomes zero or equal to the scrap value.	The value of the asset never becomes zero at any stage, but remains around its estimated scrap value.
5.	**Cost price of the asset and its entry.**	It is necessary to know the cost price of the asset to calculate the depreciation of any year because depreciation is always calculated on the cost price.	It is not necessary to know the cost price of the asset to calculate the depreciation of any year expect in the first year because depreciation is calculated on the opening balance of the asset for that year.

| 6. | *Estimate of the scrap value.* | *In order to determine the amount of depreciation the scrap value of the asset is to be ascertained, the estimate of which is difficult to make.* | *In order to determine depreciation or the rate of depreciation the scrap value of the asset is considered, but when the rate is given directly the estimate of the scrap value is not so important.* |
| 7. | *Suitable for which assets.* | *This method f is suitable for assets which have a small and definite useful life.* | *This method is suitable for assets which have a long or indefinite useful life.* |

🗋 PRACTICAL SECTION 🗋

*1) Nayan stores purchased an old machine on **1-4-01** for **Rs. 31,000** carriage and installation expenses amounted to **Rs. 4,000** repairs expenses of **Rs.5,000** were incurred on this machine before using it. Another new machine was purchased on **1-10-02** for **Rs.34,000** for which installation expenses amounted to **Rs.2,000**. The old machine purchased earlier became obsolete and was sold off on **30-9-03** at **40 %** loss on its book value. Prepare machinery account up to **31-3-04** and show the effects in the final* accounts of the year *2001-2002*. The company provides depreciation at *10%* per annum by straight line method.

2) Shivangi Service centre purchased a machine for servicing vehicles on *1-4-01* for *Rs.2,90,000.* Installation expenses amounted to *Rs.10,000* it was decided to write off depreciation on this machine at *10%* per annum by reducing balance method. This machine was sold off on *30-9-03* at *20%* loss on its book value. Prepare machinery account up to *31-3-04* and give the effects in the final accounts of the first year.

3) Jayantika corporation purchased a machine on *1-4-2000* for *Rs.1,80,000* carriage and installation expenses amounted to *Rs. 20,000* it purchased amounted to *Rs. 4,000* as the second machine was not suitable, it was sold off on *31-3-03* at *10%* profit on its book value. The company provided depreciation at *10 %* per annum by reducing balance method. Prepare machinery account up to *31-3-03* and gives the effects in final accounts of the first year.

4) The books of Vinit Corporation show an opening balance of *Rs.91,000* in the machinery account. This machine is seven years old. An amount of *Rs.49,000* has been deducted till date from the cost price of the machine as total

depreciation find out the amount of annual depreciation and the cost price of the machine.

5) *Jay Ambe corporation* *purchased some machines on **1-4-01** for **Rs.72,500** which installation expenses amounted to **Rs.7,500** It purchased some other machines on **1-10-03** for **Rs. 30,000** The company provides depreciation at **10%** per annum by fixed instalment method **70 %** of the machines purchased earlier were sold off on **31-3-04** at **20%** loss on their book value. Prepare machinery account in the books of the company up to **31-3-04**.*

6) *Saumil industries* *purchases a machine on **1-4-01** for **Rs. 1,06,000** installation expenses amounted to **Rs.14,000** it purchases another machine on **1-4-02** for **Rs.56,000** for which installation expenses amounted to **Rs.4,000** the first machine was sold off an **31-3-04** at **20%** profit on its book value. The company provided depreciation at **10%** per annum by reducing balance method. Prepare machinery account up to **31-3-04** and show the effects in the final accounts of the year **2002-03**.*

7) *King Limited* *purchased a machine on **1-4-01** for **Rs.1,44,000** installation expenses amounted to **Rs.6,000** it purchased another machine on **1-1-03** for **Rs.36,000** The company provides depreciation at **10%** per annum by reducing balance method. The company sold off the second machine on **31-3-04** at **20 %** loss on its book value. Prepare machinery account.*

8) **Toral enterprise** *purchased machines of* **Rs. 46,000** *on* **1-4-01**. *Installation expenses amounted to* **Rs. 4,000** *The company purchases other machines of* **Rs.32,500** *on* **1-4-03** *as per its requirements. It provides depreciation at* **10%** *per annum by reducing balance method. On* **30-9-03, 50%** *of the machines purchased earlier were sold off at* **20%** *profit on their book value. prepare machinery account up to* **31-3-04.**

...........xxxxxxxxx.........

CHAPTER –3

("Reserve and Contingences ")

◻ THEORY SECTION ◻

❖ Reserve :

"Reserve means the amount allocated from the profit in order to face a certain or an uncertain expense, loss or liability in the future. This reserve is created from profit and loss appropriation account. A reserve created in this manner may be for a define purpose or for maintaining the solvency of the business."

❖ Objectives of a Reserve :

The objectives for creating a reserve in a business are as follows :

(1) If there is a big loss in the future or some unexpected expense is payable, it becomes possible to face such an unexpected contingency.

(2) In order that a certain liability of the business payable in the future can be paid easily, a specific reserve may also be created.

(3) It strengthens the liquidity position for the solvency of the business.

❖ *Provision :*

   "Provision is an amount allocated from the profit with the purpose of preparation for the payment of a certain liability whose amount cannot be determined e.g. provision for depreciation or depreciation fund. Provision for doubtful debts or bad debts reserve, repairs reserve, provision for claims debenture redemption reserve, provision for income tax etc."

❖ *Objectives of a provision :*

The objectives of provision in a business are as follows :

(1) *To make financial arrangements against a probable loss in the future e.g. for bad debts by bad debts reserve. For depreciation by depreciation fund.*

(2) *To make sufficient fanatical arrangements for known expenses of the business whose payment amount is not certain and can be written off against such a provision e.g. repairs reserve.*

(3) *To make economic arrangement for the modernization of the business e.g. modernization reserve.*

(4) *To create a fund of to arrange finance for payment of a certain liability in the future e.g. debenture redemption reserve.*

❖ *Types of reserve :*
(1) **Revenue reserve :**

The profit which arises from the purchase and sale of goods and such other activities of the business is known as revenue profit.

Revenue profit reserve is very useful for improving the solvency of the business when there is no definite or special purpose for creating this reserve, it is known as general reserve, this reserve is created out of the profit of the business from the profit and loss appropriation account.

❖ **Main objectives of revenue reserve :** *The main objectives of creating a revenue reserve in a business are as follows :*

a) **To meet expenses and losses :** *there are various types of expenses and losses in a business but when a big amount is to be paid for an expense or a loss, revenue reserve can be useful.*

b) **For solvency of the business :** *reserve is created to improve the capacity to meet business uncertainties, which reflects the solvency of the business. The more the free reserves of a business, the greater is its solvency.*

c) **To face unexpected expenses :** *accidental loss or large expenses or unexpected situation are the testing time for any business. A reserve becomes useful to meet any such accidental large expenses of the business in future.*

[31]

(2) ***General Reserve*** *: this is also a type of revenue reserve there is no definite purpose for creating the general reserve. However, its main aim is to increase the economic solvency of the business. No definite expenses is associated with this reserve. In short general reserve is like an anchor during bad times. General reserve is created from the profit and loss appropriation account.*

❖ ***Main objectives of general reserve : the general reserve is created keeping in mind the following objectives :***

   a) ***To strengthen the financial position of the business :*** *when the business earns sufficient profit, if a certain part of the profit is taken to the reserve, the profit remains in the business and the business gets additional working capital to that extent. It helps the business like a fuel, hence, this reserve is necessary to make the financial position of the business stronger.*

   b) ***To face unexpected circumstances :*** *the business should be capable to face any kind of economic problem in order to face any unexpected situation an arrangement in the form of this reserve is necessary for the business.*

c) **To maintain stability in dividend :** *the goodwill of a company is directly associated with the dividend declared every year due to any reason if less profit is earned in my year, dividend will have to be declared at a lower rate which will have an adverse effect on the goodwill of the company.*

d) **To declare bonus shares :** *when a certain amount is transferred to general reserve every year, there will be a large amount accumulated in the reserve after few years. now when a large amount is collected as general reserve, the company can issue bonus shares to its shareholders by capitalizing the reserve, so that the goodwill of the company can be increased.*

e) **To strengthen the liquidity position of the business :** *a business can run easily if it has sufficient working capital and liquidity. Current liabilities or any other additional liability can be paid without any difficulty during an accounting year.*

f) **For future development of the business :** *a business can become self-dependent to a large extent for its development by re-investing the profit in the business through this reserve.*

g) **Reserve fund :** *normally, the amount in general reserve remains in the business in the form of working capital. But if the amount in this reserve is* *invested in investments outside the business, then general reserve is known as reserve fund.*

A company creates a dividend equalization fund or balancing the rates of dividend.

(3) ***Special reserve or provision :*** *when a reserve is created for a specific purpose, it is known as special reserve or provision, an important point here is that this reserve can be used for that purpose only for which it is created e.g. reserve for doubtful debts.*

Moreover, these provisions have to be compulsorily whether there is a profit or a loss at the end of a year because the concerned expenses or losses are unavoidable.

At this juncture, let us understand that there is one difference between special reserve and provision when the future liability or loss is known and the amount is also certain, then the reserve created for it is known as special reserve e.g. debenture redemption reserve. When the future liability or loss is known but the amount is not certain, then the reserve for it is known as a provision e.g. reserve for doubtful debts.

The amount of provision can be used for the decided purpose only, but when the purpose of such a reserve is over, the balance amount of the provision may be transferred to the profit & loss account or the general reserve and used for any other purpose.

Special reserve or provision is created from the profit and loss account.

Considering debenture redemption reserve as an appropriation it is appropriated from proft & loss appropriation account (from the profit) for that, the amount is debited to profit and loss appropriation account and credited to debenture redemption reserve account the entry is as follows :

Profit & loss appropriation A/c   Dr.
                    To debenture redemption reserve A/c
(being profit appropriated to debenture redemption reserve)

❖ ***Objectives of special reserve or provision :*** *The objectives of creating special reserve or provision are as under :*

a) ***Provision for certain expenses of future :*** *if provision is made every year for certain large expenses losses or liability to take place in the future, when such expenses are actually to be borne, there is no adverse effect on the running business e.g. provision for taxation.*

b) ***For uncertain expenses or losses of future :*** *some expenses and losses in a business are such whose amount cannot be determined with certainly. E.g. bad debts.*

c) For outstanding expenses : at the end of an accounting year, certain expenses of the business are yet to be paid. E.g. unpaid salary, unpaid rent et.

(4) Capital reserve :

Reserve created out of capital profit is capital reserve. Profit arising due to revaluation of assets, profit received on sale of assets, premium received on issue of share or debentures etc. are considered capital profits of a business. Capital reserve is created from this profit. For this the amount of capital profit is transferred to capital reserve account.

❖ *Source(situations) of capital profit :* capital reserve can be created with the help of capital profit earned in the following situations :

(1) Profit received on sale of a fixed asset at a price higher than the cost of the asset

(2) Additional amount on revaluation of a fixed asset at a higher price is a capital profit. (revaluation reserve)

(3) Profit of a company prior to incorporation.

(4) Premium received on issue of shares or debentures.

(5) Balance amount in share forfeiture account after the reissue of forfeited shares.

(6) On purchase of running business, when the price paid is less than the price of the net assets.

(7) On redemption of debentures when the amount repaid is less than the book value of the debentures.

❖ ***Uses of capital reserve : capital reserve can be used for the following purpose :***

a) *This reserve can be used for writing off capital losses like loss on revaluation of assets, loss on sale of fixed assets etc.*

b) *This reserve can be used for writing off fictitious or intangible assets like goodwill, preliminary expenses, discount on shares or debenture etc.*

c) *Generally, dividend is declared out of revenue profits. But in special circumstances under special conditions dividend can be declared out of capital reserve also.*

d) *Bonus shares can be issued to the shareholders from capital reserve if there is a precision in the company's acridities of association.*

*(5) **Sinking fund :** a company creates special reserve for repayment of a long term loan or for repayment of a long term liability like debentures or for purchase of new assets to replace old inefficient assets, which is known as a sinking fund.*

*(6) **Secret Reserve :** there is no reserve with such a name in the books of accounts. But the business assets, receivables, liabilities, provisions etc. are shown in*

such a way that secretly a reserve comes into existence. By wringing off more depreciation on the assets or by making more provision for expected liabilities, less profit is shown in the books, which in my reality is more such additional depreciation or provision for liabilities is a secret reserve.

☆ **Difference between : General reserve and Provision**

General Reserve	Provision (special Reserve)
Objectives : *general reserve is created not for any specific purpose but for the economic solvency of the business*	***Objectives :*** *Provision is a financial arrangement created for a specific purpose like provision for depreciation.*
Appropriation from which account : *general reserve is appropriated from profit & loss appropriation account.*	***Appropriation from which account :*** *Provision is appropriated from profit & loss account*
Only if there is a profit (voluntary) : *general reserve is appropriated only if there is a profit at the end of the accounting year*	***Even if there is loss (compulsory):****it is necessary or compulsory to make a provision even if there is a loss at the end of the accounting year.*
Use : *general reserve can be used for any purpose*	***Use :*** *provision can be used only for that purpose for which provision has been made.*

Appropriation of amount : the amount to be appropriated from the profit to general reserve account depends on the amount of annual profit, opinion of the management, law etc. when instructed by law, reserve ore reserves have to be created in the same way	*Appropriation of amount :* the amount for provision is normally certain, or a specific amount or percentage is decided on the basis of the estimate depending on past experience.
Effect in the balance sheet : the amount of general reserve is shown under the heading reserves and surplus on the liabilities side of the balance sheet.	*Effect in the balance sheet :* the amount of provision is either deducted from the concerned asset in the balance sheet or shown under the heading provisions on the capital and liabilities side.
Writing off loses : since general reserve is a profit shown separately, loss of a year can be written off against the general reserve	*Writing off loses :* provision cannot be used for writing off loss of a year.

☆ *Difference between : General reserve and Capital reserve.*

General Reserve	*Capital reserve*
Revenue profit : *general reserve is the revenue profit of the business it is created from the revenue profit.*	**Capital profit :** *capital reserve is the capital profit of the business, because amount of capital profit is taken to capital reserve account.*
For solvency : *general reserve increases the economic solvency of the business and helps to face unexpected loses.*	**For maintaining capital profit:** *as the capital profit of the business defers from the general reserve, it can normally be used special circumstances.*
Use (for dividend) : *general reserve in a company can be used for declaring and distributing divided.*	**Use (for divided) :** *capital reserve cannot be used for declaring divided in normal circumstances. However, there is not prohibition on using capital profits for declaring dividends in the companies act. But for that, certain restrictive provisions have to be followed however, capital reserve created by revaluation of assets and liabilities cannot be used for declaring dividend.*

Many uses : as general reserve is not limited to any specific purpose, it is vast. As general reserve is the amount of profit, it has many uses as the uses of profit e.g. writing off losses, distributing dividend, issuing bonus shares etc.	Limited uses : the use of capital reserve is limited this reserve can be used to write off fictitious assets, to write off capital losses and if there is a provision in the articles of association to issue bonus shares.

.............×××××××××.........

CHAPTER –4

("Non-trading Concerns")

☐ THEORY SECTION ☐

❖ *Meaning and characteristics of non-trading concerns :*

The institutions which come into existence not with an intention to earn profit, but they exist for social services, welfare of its members protection and development of the right of its members, expansion of sports and education, development of cultural activities etc. are known as non trading concerns. Such concerns receive income from their activities but their object is not to earn profit. their object is to achieve physical, mental, intellectual and religious development of their members and society, by providing services.

These intuitions include hospital, library, school, college, orphanage, religious institution, charitable intuition, institution of sports gymkhana, association of traders, labour union etc e.g. Gujarat Vidhyapith, Jivansadhana school, rotary club, lions club, chamber of commerce, polo club etc.

♣ *Characteristics :*

characteristics of non-trading concerns are as below :

(1)   The main motive of this institutions, is not to earn profit but to render the services.

(2)   As such institutions do not come into existence either for trading activities, or for producing, purchasing or selling the goods and therefore they trading account and profit-loss a/c. but sometimes intuitions like sports clubs etc, in order to facilitate their members, provide (sales) the goods by purchasing them from the market. Some institutions provide the services like canteen too.

(3)   At the end of the year it does not prepare profit and loss a/c as its main motive is not to earn profits. But to know the status of incomes and expenses it prepares income-expenditure a/c.

(4)   Generally, proportion of cash transactions remains more in this institution and therefore it prepares receipt-payment a/c, to record the cash transactions.

(5)   Capital of non-trading concern is known as capital fund or permanent fund.

(6)   At the end of the year, in order to know the fininicial position it prepares balance sheet.

(7)   Main source of income of this institution is subscription from members in addition thereto, it also receives income by way of donation, govt. aid, interest on investments, dividend, income of charity etc.

❖ ***Accounts of non-trading concerns :*** *there are two types of accounting system.*

1. **Mercantile system** : *according to this system, accounts are prepared after taking into consideration unpaid expenses and incomes not received in addition to expenses paid and incomes received during the year. Non trading concerns prepare accounts as per this system.*

2. **Cash system** : *according to this system, accounts, are prepared considering only the expenses paid and incomes received during the year.*

   As non-trading concerns prepare their accounts as per mercantile system mainly it prepares accounts as under.

3. **Receipt and payment account :** *cash and bank balances as well as cash receipt and cash payments are recorded in this account. Its nature is similarly to that of cash account.*

4. **Income and expenditure account :** *this account is similar to profit and loss of a trading concern. Only revenue incomes and revenue expenses of current year, are recorded. Result of this account i.e. excess of income over expenses is added to capital fund and if it is excess of expenses over incomes, is deducted from capital fund in balance sheet.*

5. **Balance sheet :** *at the end of a year, to know the financial position non-trading concern prepares balance sheet. Capital of this concern is known as capital fund or permanent fund. Other particulars (assets, receipt, due,*

advance paid amounts, liabilities and unpaid amounts). Are similar to the balance sheet of a trading concern, sometimes accumulated amount of income-expenditure a/c is shown separately in the balance sheet.

❖ **Difference between the account of trading and non-trading concerns**

Trading concerns	Non- trading concerns
Meaning : *those concerns having an object of earning profit from sale and purchase of goods and from other trading activities are known as trading concerns.*	*Those institutions which do not have an object to earn profit but to render services and social welfare are known as non trading concerns. There may be a possibility of sales and purchase of goods to fulfill such objectives of rendering services.*
Trading a/c : *at the end of a year, to find our gross profit or loss, it prepares trading a/c*	*Generally, as it is not engaged in sales and purchases of goods, it is not preparing trading a/c but an account similar to it, income expenditure a.c is prepared.*
P & L A/c : *to know the result of a business it prepares profit and loss a/c*	*It prepares income expenditure a/c to know incomes and expenses arising from various activities of the concern.*
Result of a business concern : *result of trading concern is*	*Result of non-trading concern is known as ' excess of income*

known as net profit or net loss.	*over expenses' or excess of expenses over incomes*
Income : *main source of income is sale of goods.*	*Main source of income are membership fees, subscription donation etc.*
Capital-fund : *excess of assets over liabilities is known as capital*	*Excess of assets over liabilities is known as capital fund of permanent fund.*
Accounting system : *trading concerns maintain its books of accounts on mercantile system.*	*Non trading concerns also maintain its books of accounts as per mercantile system only. Therein receipt payment a/c, income expenditure a/c and balance sheet are three main important statements. Sometimes accumulated balance of income expenditure a/c is shown separately in the balance sheet. Accumulated credit balance of income expenditure a/c is shown after adding current year's excess of income over expenses and after deducting excess of expenses over incomes, if any.*

❖ ***Classification of incomes :***

There are two types of receipt of an institution.

(1) ***Capital income :*** *The income which is received by the institution not regularly or reputedly as well as those incomes the benefit of which is going to be received by the institution for a longer period are known as capital income e.g. legacy received life membership subscription. Donation received for specific purpose borrowed loan etc.*

Generally, in non-trading concerns except borrowing capital incomes such as donation, legacy etc. are added in capital fund.

(2) ***Revenue income :*** *The income arising from the routine activities of an institutions and is received regularly by the institutions is known as revenue income e.g. annual subscriptions of members, interest is known as revenue of old news papers, income from entertainment programmed, income of entertainment programme, income of rent of sports ground, lockers rent, income or profit arising from providing services with charge etc. in non-trading concerns revenue incomes are shown on the credit side of income-expenditure account.*

❖ ***Difference between Capital income and Revenue income :***

Capital income	*Revenue income*
Meaning : *the income which is not received by the institution regularly or repeatedly as well as the*	*The income which is received regularly and which arises from the routine activities of an institution, is known as*

income, benefit of which is going to be received for a longer period is known as capital income	revenue income.
Object : object is to receive long term fund.	Object is to earn regular income.
Presentation in accounts : it is shown on the liabilities side of a balance sheet.	**It is known on the credit side of income expenditure a/c.**
Balance : every year balance of capital income account is carried forward.	As the revenue income accounts are closed at the end of a year, by transferring them to income expenditure a/c there remains no balance to be carried forward.
Information obtained : it gives an idea regarding financial position of an institution	It gives an regarding day-today incomes of an institution and there by its increase of decrease is known.
Illustration : legacy, donation for specific purpose, charity, income form sale of assets etc.	Subscriptions, lockers rent, sale of old news papers etc.

❖ *Classification of expenses :*

Expenses of a non-trading concern can be classified into three types.

a) **Capital expenditure :** *expense which is not incurred regularly or repeatedly and the benefit of which is received by the institution for a longer period as well* *as because of which fixed asset is acquired by an institution, is known as capital expenditure. E.g. land, building, furniture, machinery investments, books for library, x-ray machine, sports equipments swimming pool etc.*

b) ***Revenue expenditure*** : *expense which is incurred to carry on day to day activities of an institution, to maintain the assets in proper and efficient condition or the expense whose benefit is going to be received by the institution for the current year only is known as revenue expense. E.g. day-to day administration expenses like employee's salary. Rent, taxes postage-telegrams, subscription for news papers, repairs for assets, depreciation of assets, ground maintenance expenses etc.*

Revenue expenses are shown on the debit side of income expenditure a/c.

❖ ***Difference between Capital expenditure and Revenue expenditure***

Capital expenditure	*Revenue expenditure*
Meaning : *expense which is not incurred regularly or repeatedly and the benefit of which is received by the institution for a longer period as well as because of which fixed asset is acquired by an*	*Expense which is incurred regularly and respectably to carry on day-to day activities of an institution, which is necessary to maintain the asset in efficient condition and the*

institution is known as capital expenditure.	benefit of which is going to be received by the institution for the current year only is revenue expenditure.
Object : the object of capital expenditure is to acquire fixed assets and with the help of which to create facilities or to generate income.	The object is to carry on day-to-day activities of the institution.
Presentation in accounts : it is shown on assets side in a balance sheet.	It is known on debt side in income expenditure a/c.
Presentation in accounts balance : after deducting deprecation thereon remaining balance is carried forward.	Balance is not carried forward but is closed by transferring it to income-expenditure A/c.
Benefit of expenditure is received for a long period. Fixed assets- land, building machinery furniture purchased installation charged paid etc.	Benefit is received for that particular year only. Day-to day administrative expenses such as salary, post-telegram expenses, repairing expense etc.

☆ Deferred Revenue Expenditure :

The benefit of a revenue expenditure is received only in the year in which it is incurred but there are certain expenses, the benefit of which is received not only in the year in which is incurred but is also extended to subsequent year.

Therefore instead of debiting such expenses entirely in the year in which they are incurred as revenue expenditure, written off by allocating the same proportionately over a number of years. such type of expenses are known as differed revenue expenditure.

❖ *Revenue expenditure and differed revenue expenditure :*

Revenue expenditure	Differed revenue expenditure
Meaning : *expense, the benefit of which is received by the institution for that respective accounting year only id a revenue expenditure*	*Expenses of which the benefit is received by the institution for more than one accounting year, is a differed revenue expenditure*
Object : *its object is to carry on day-to day activities of a business*	*As the benefit is received for more than one accounting year, the object is to know correct result of the business by writing it off proportionately over some years.*
Presentation in accounts : *it is shown on the debit side of income-expenditure account*	*Out of this the portion which is written off is shown on the debit side of income-expenditure a/c and that portion which is not written off is shown on the assets side in balance sheet.*
Balance : *no balance is carried forward but account is closed by transferring it to income expenditure a/c*	*The amount which is not written off, is carried forward.*
Amount of expense written	*Total amount of differed*

off : total amount of revenue expense is written off in one year only.	revenue expenditure is written off pro-portionately during some years.
Illustrations : day to day administrative expenses and monetary expenses like salary, rent, stationery, bank interest etc.	Preliminary expenses, discount or underwriting commission given at the time of issue of shares or debentures, large scale advertisement campaign expenses.

☆ Clarification of certain item in the accounts of non-trading concern and its accounting effects.

(1) **Capital fund or permanent fund :** from income expenditure account the excess of incomes over expenses is added to capital fund and excess of expenses over incomes is deducted from capital fund. Sometimes instead of adding the excess of income and deducting excess of expenses from capital fund, it is shown separately on accumulated basis in the balance sheet on the liabilities side and current year's excess of income is added therein and excess of expenses is deducted there from excess of incomes and excess of expenses are also known as surplus and deficiency respectively.

(2) **Subscription or membership fees :** specified amount is paid regularly every year by the members of the

institution to continue their membership. For institution this is a revenue income.

*(3) **Admission fees or entrance fees :** at the time of taking admission as a member in the institution for the first time. New members have to pay admission or entrance fees. Income of such admission or entrance fees should be treated as either capital income or revenue income as decided by the rules and regulations of the by laws of an institution. In the absences of clarification, entrance fees should be treated as a revenue income only.*

*(4) **Life membership :** some members of the intuition become life members by paying specific lump sum as determined by the by laws of the institution, instead of paying annual membership fees.*

*(5) **Donation :** generally donation is considering as a capital income and thus it is added to capital fund. If the institution gets regular donations, then it is treated as revenue income.*

*(6) **Legacy :** some persons give their property through will to the institution as legacy. Such type of legacy received is shown as an addition in the capital fund, considered as a capital income.*

*(7) **Fund or specific purpose :** when a fund is created for any specific purpose, all expenses related to that fund are deducted there from and all incomes relating to that fund is added therein. A fund created for specific*

purpose are shown in balance sheet on liabilities side, separately, from capital fund. E.g. prize fund, president's felicitation fund etc.

If the amount of expenses relating to a specific fund is more than the amount of that fund, such excess will be treated as revenue expenditure and is debited to income- expenditure account.

❖ **Receipt-payment account :**

Meaning :

In non-trading institution, generally proportion of cash transactions remains more. A summary prepared by non-trading institution of cash receipt and cash payments during the year is known as receipt- payment a/c. this account is a short summary of cash transactions during the year. On its debit side cash receipt and on credit side cash payments are recorded. In addition to cash transactions, bank transactions are also recorded in this account, its nature is similar to cash amount.

Specimen of receipt- payment account receipt-payment a/c for the year ending on......

Receipt	Amount Rs.	Payments	Amount Rs.
Opening cash / bank balance	....	Opening bank overdraft	....
Current year's past year's and next	....	Current year's past year's and	....

year's revenue and capital incomes, received in cash		next year's income and capital expenses paid in cash	
Cash withdrawn from bank Closing bank overdraft	… … … … .... … … … …	Cash deposited in bank Closing cash /bank balance	… … … … .... … … … … ....

❖ **Income-expenditure account :** *the account which is prepared by non-trading institution at the end of the year to know the result (surplus/ deficit) of the intuition, is known as income-expenditure a/c. on the debit side of this account current year's revenue expenses and on the credit side current year's revenue incomes are recorded. This account is similar to profit and loss account of trading concern. In order to meet day-to-day expenses of an institutions, whether sufficient incomes are there or not, can be known with the help of income-expenditure account.*

Specimen of income-expenditure account

Particulars	Amount	Particulars	Amount
Current year's revenue expenses : Paid in cash during current year ….….. +unpaid for current year ….…..		Current year's revenue income : Received in cash during the year ….….. + outstanding of	

+prepaid in last year …….. - Unpaid of past year paid during the year ………. - Paid in advance for next year, during the year ……… depreciation		current year ………. +received in advance in last year ……. -outstanding of last received during the year ……. -received in advance for next year excess over incomes (deficit)	
Loss on sale of assets excess of income over expenses (surplus)			

❖ **Difference between Receipt- payment a/c and Income expenditure a/c**

Receipt- payment account	Income-expenditure account
Meaning : a summary prepared by non-trading institution, of cash receipt and cash payments effected during the year, is known as receipt payment a/c	An account prepared by non-trading institution at the end of the year to know the result of the institution, is known as income expenditure a/c.

Nature : *it is similar to cash account*	*It is similar to profit-loss a/c*
Opening balance : *cash balance, bank balance or bank over draft is its opening balance.*	*No opening balance is there in this account.*
Closing balance : *closing balance of this a/c is a closing cash balance, bank balance or bank overdraft*	*Closing balance of this a/c is either excess of incomes over expenses or excess of expenses over incomes.*
Recording of closing balance : *if the closing balance is a cash balance, or bank balance, it is shown on the assets side in balance sheet and if closing balance is a bank overdraft, it is shown on the liabilities side in balance sheet.*	*If closing balance of this a/c is excess of incomes over expenses it will be added in capital fund in balance sheet and if closing balance is excess of expenses over incomes it will be deducted from capital fund in balance sheet sometimes accumulated balance of income expenditure a/c is shown separately in balance sheet.*
Capital and revenue income and expenses : *classification of capital and revenue is not necessary for both incomes and expenses. Both types of receipt and payments effected in cash, are recorded in this a/c*	*Only revenue incomes and revenue expenses are recorded in this a/c. capital income and capital expenses are recorded in balance sheet.*
Time : *receipt and payments*	*Only current year's revenue*

are of which year is immaterial, though it is for current year, past year, or next year, but if in cash, it is recorded in this account.	income and revenue expenses are recorded in this account. Incomes received and expenses paid for past year
Non-cash transactions : as this account is prepared on cash basis, depreciation, bad debts, incomes not received un paid expenses etc. are not recorded in this account.	As this account is prepared on mercantile basis, depreciation adjustments regarding bad debt, incomes not received, unpaid expenses etc. are recorded in this account.
Balance sheet : it is not necessary to prepare balance sheet with this account.	Preparation of balance sheet is necessary after preparing this account.

☐ PRACTICAL SECTION ☐

1. From the following information prepare receipt-payment a/c and income-expenditure a/c of **of Baroda cricket club** for the year ending on **31-3-2004.**

Particulars	Amount	Particulars	Amount
Cash balance (1-4-03)	16,000	Tournament fees received	84,000
Bank overdraft	12,000	Ground maintained expenses	16,000
Subscription from		Donation received	60,000

members : 2003-2004 : 5,000 2004-2005 : __45,000__	50,000	Honorarium to secretary	24,000
		Sale of souvenirs	40,000
Remuneration to cricket coach	20,000	Donation received for tournament	72,000
Salary of grounds man	10,000	Tournament fund investment	80,000
Purchase of sports Equipments	68,000	Poetry conference expenses	20,000
Entrance fees	20,000	Stationery expenses	8,000
Subscription received		Repairing expenses	8,000
From participants in sports	14,000	Bank interest received	1,600
Expenses to prepare wicket	10,000	Tournament expenses	60,000
Tournament prize	32,000	Umpire' fees	12,000
Distribution expenses		Affiliation fee with main club	4,000
Income from poetry		Taxes- insurance	4,000
Conference	40,000	Interest on tournament fund investments	20,000
Souvenir printing expenses	12,000	Cash balance (31-3-04)	1,600
		Bank balance (31-3- 04)	16,00 0

Additional information :

(1) subscription of Rs.4,000 is outstanding from the members participating in sports.

(2)Subscription of Rs.2000 is outstanding for the current year from the members.

(3)Inclusive in insurance premium Rs.1,200 is paid in advance.

(4)75% of entrance fee is to be capitalized.

2. **Income expenditure a/c for the year ending on 31-3-2004 and a balance sheet as on that date.**

Particulars	Rs.	Particulars	Rs.
To balance b/f (1-4-2003 bank balance as on)	17,500	By salary	32,500
		By rent-taxes	4,500
To subscription :		By stationery purchase	2,250
2002-03 450		By purchase of sports Equipments (1-10-03)	15,000
2003-04 43,500			
2004-05 300	44,250	By sundry expenses	6,000
		12% bank deposited(w.e.f. 1-1-2004)	
To income from entertainment	10,000		
To interest on 12% Investments (of 12 months)	3,000		12,500

		(w.e.f) wirth effect from	
		by expenses of entertainment	
To donation	**5,000**	*programmed*	**5,300**
To entrance fee	**1,000**	*Balance c/f*	**3,000**
To sale of old news		**(bank balance on**	
papers	**300**	**31-3-2004)**	
	1,62,100		**1,62,100**

Additional information :

1) *in a club there are total **Rs.150** members each paying annual subscription of **Rs.150**.*

2) *opening capital fund is **Rs.65,700**.*

3) *outstanding salary as on **31-3-2003** is **Rs.2,500** and on **31-3-2004** is and **Rs. 3,750** respectively.*

4) *Opening and closing stock of stationery is **Rs.250** and **Rs.375** respectively.*

5) *Sports equipments are worth **Rs.25,000** and **Rs.35,000** as on **1-4-2003** and **31-3-2004** respectively.*

3. *From the following receipt payment a/c for the year ending on **31-3-2004** of **Apollo hospital** and other additional information provided, prepare its income expenditure a/c and balance sheet.*
   Receipt payment a/c for the year ending on 31-3-2004 of Apollo hospital.

receipts	Amount Rs.	payments	Amount Rs.
To opening cash balance	12,000	By construction expenses of operation theatre	2,40,000
To subscription	3,00,000	By purchase of medicines	1,68,000
To donation	1,50,000	By honorarium to doctors	1,50,000
To interest on investments	30,000	By salary	1,08,000
To income from hospital	60,000	By sundry expenses	3,000
To specific donation for operation theatre	3,00,000	By purchase of equipment	1,32,000
To government aid	90,000	By expenses of hospital	18,000
To sale of old papers	3,000	By subscription of periodicals	18,000
		By fixed deposit in bank	90,000
		By closing cash balance	18,000
	9,45,000		9,45,000

Additional information :

particulars	As on 1-4-2003 Rs.	As on 31-3-2004 Rs
Outstanding subscription to receive	1,800	3000
Subscription received in advance	600	1200
Stock of medicines	36,000	42,000
Equipments	2,10,000	3,12,000
Building less depreciation	2,40,000	2,28,000
Investment	1,50,000	1,50,000
Capital fund	6,49,200	?

4. From the following information prepare income expenditure a/c for the year ending **31-3-2004** and balance sheet as on that date of **Satnam sports club.**

Balance sheet as on 31-3-2003

liabilities	Amount Rs.	assets	Amount Rs.
Capital fund	51,000	Furniture	5,000
Excess of income over expenses	6,000	Sports equipments	30,000
Subscription received in advance	1,000	10 % investments	20,000
		Subscription outstanding	3,000
Outstanding salary	2,000	Prepaid rent	500
		Cash balance	1,500
	60,000		60,000

Receipt payment a/c for the year ending on 31-3- 2004

particulars	Amount	particulars	Amount
To balance c/d	1,500	By salary	8,000
To entrance fee	2,000	By rent	4,500
		By sports equipments (dt 1-10-2003)	10,000
To subscription	25,000		
To interest on investment	1,500	By subscription for periodical	1,000
To donation	2,500	By sundry expenses	1,500
To sale of old newspapers	400	Balance c/f	8,000
To sundry income	100		
	33,000		33,000

Additional information :

1) At the end of the year, subscription of **Rs.6,000** is yet to received for the current year.

2) At the end of the year, unpaid salary is **Rs.1000.**

3) Subscription received includes **Rs.2,000** for the year of **2004-05**

4) Provide depreciation on furniture and sports equipments at **10%** and **20%** respectively.

5) Capitalize half of entrance fees.

5. *From the following information, prepare income expenditure a/c for the year end on **31-3-2004** and a balance sheet as on that date, in the books of **Patel Samaj**. Balance on **31-3-2003** balances as on :*

Building **Rs.2,00,000**

unpaid salary **Rs.12,000**

capital fund **Rs.4,00,000**

excess of income over expenses **Rs.56,000**

12 % national savings certificates **Rs.1,00,000**

subscription received in advance **Rs.4,000**

loan borrowed at **10% Rs.1,60,000**

due but not received subscription **Rs.20,000.**

Receipt payment a/c for the year ending 31-3-2004

Receipts	Amount	Payments	Amount
To balance c/d	12,000	By salary	60,000
		By subscription for periodicals	12,000
To subscriptions :			
2002-2003 20,000		By general expenses	8,000
		By stationery printing	6,000
2003-2004 1,00,000			
2004-2005 8,000	1,28,000	By interest on loan	12,000
To interest on investments	12,000	By repairing expenses	24,000
To entrance fees	16,000	By electricity exp.	16,000

To donation	32,000	By expenses for social gathering	36,000
To income of social gatherings	1,00,000	By extension in building	88,000
To sale of old newspapers	2,000	By snacks expenses	10,000
To lockers rent	6,000	By balance c/f	36,000
	3,08,000		3,08,000

Other information :

1) Capitalize **80 %** of entrance fees.

2) Subscription of **Rs.12,000** is outstanding for the year of **2003-2004.**

3) Salary of **Rs.8,000** is unpaid.

4) Write off **Rs. 44,000** for depreciation on building

5) Unpaid electricity expenses is **Rs.4,000.**

6. From the following information of **Karnavati club,** prepare its income expenditure account, and receipt-payment a/c for the year ending **31-3-2004** and a balance sheet as on that date.

Balance as on **1-4-2003**

capital fund **Rs.4,00,000**

excess of income over expenses **Rs.80,000**

sports equipment **Rs.1,20,000**

subscription received in advance **Rs.24,000**

subscription outstanding **Rs.36,000**

unpaid ground rent **Rs.36,000**

cash on hand **Rs.24,000**

office building Rs. 3,60,000.

Cash transactions for the year 2003-2004

Receipts	Amount	Payments	Amount
Subscription received	6,00,000	Miscellaneous income	48,000
Salary	1,80,000	Electricity expenses	60,000
Honorarium to manager	1,08,000	Stationery printing	12,000
Ground rent	2,40,000	Postage expenses	6,000
Expenses for annual dinner	1,32,000	Repairing expenses	36,000
Entrance fees	36,000	Contribution of annual dinner	1,80,000
Purchase of furniture	96,000	Donation	2,04,000
		Purchase of spots equipments	1,20,000

Other information :

1) inclusive in subscription **Rs.36,000** is received for the year **2004-2005.**

2) Subscription outstanding is received **Rs.60,000** for the year **2004-005.**

3) Ground rent unpaid is **Rs.12,000**

4) **50 %** of entrance fee is to be capitalized

5) Provide **10 %** depreciation on the closing balance of building, furniture and sports equipments.

...........××××××××××.........

CHAPTER – 5

"ACCOUNTING RATIO"

FORMULA

⇒ <u>**Profitability Ratios**</u> **:**

1) *Gross Profit Ratio* $= \dfrac{Gross\ Profit}{Sales}$ *x **100***

> ➢ *Gross Profit = Sales – Cost of goods sold*

> ➢ *Cost of goods sold = Opening stock + purchase + purchase expenses – closing stock*

2) *Net Profit Ratio* $= \dfrac{Net\ Profit\,(After\ Tax)}{Sales}$ *x **100***

Net Profit (before interest and tax)	----------
Less : interest on debenture	----------
Net Profit (before and tax)	----------
Less : tax	----------
Net Profit (After Tax)	----------

3) *Operating Ratio*

$$= \dfrac{Cost\ of\ goods\ sold + Operating\ expenses}{Sales}\ x\ \textbf{100}$$

> ➢ *Cost of goods sold = Opening stock + purchase + purchase expenses – closing stock*

➢ *Cost of goods sold = Sales – Gross Profit*

❖ *Operating expenses includes Administrative expenses, selling and distribution expenses, depreciation but does not include financial expenses (interest) and provision for taxation.*

⇒ **Liquidity Ratios :**

4) *Current Ratio* $= \dfrac{\text{Current Assets}}{\text{Current Liabilities}}$

❖ *Current Assets includes debtors, bills receivable, closing stock, cash balance, bank balance, prepaid expenses, short term investments, loose tools etc.*

❖ *Current Liabilities includes creditors, bills payable, bank overdraft, outstanding expenses, workers' saving account, provident fund, workers' profit sharing fund, outstanding expenses, provision for taxes etc.*

5) *Liquid Ratio* $= \dfrac{\text{Liquid Assets}}{\text{Liquid Liabilities}}$

❖ *Liquid Assets includes all current assets except closing stock*

❖ *Liquid Liabilities includes all current liabilities except bank overdraft*

⇒ **Activity Ratios :**

6) *Stock turnover Ratio* $= \dfrac{\text{Cost of goods sold}}{\text{Average Stock}}$

$$\text{Average Stock} = \dfrac{\text{Opening Stock} + \text{Closing Stock}}{2}$$

**** when only closing stock and sales information is given at that time :

$$\text{Stock turnover Ratio} = \dfrac{sales}{\text{closing Stock}}$$

7) *Debtors Ratio*

$$= \dfrac{\text{Debtors} + \text{Bills receivable}}{\text{Credit Sales}} \; x \; \text{No.of working days}$$

8) *Creditors Ratio* $= \dfrac{\text{Creditors} + \text{Bills payable}}{\text{Credit Purchase}} \; x \; No.of\ working\ days$

9) **Working Capital Turnover Ratio**

(A) *Based on Net Working Capital*

$$\text{Working Capital Turnover} = \dfrac{Sales}{\text{Net Working Capital}}$$

❖ *Net Working Capital = Total Current Assets - Total Current Liabilities*

(B) <u>*Based on Gross Working Capital / Based on Total Current Assets*</u>

$$\text{Working Capital Turnover} = \frac{Sales}{Gross\ Working\ Capital}$$

❖ *Gross Working Capital = Total Current Assets*

<u>*Note*</u> *: When there is no specific instruction, calculation of working capital turnover is expected based on* <u>*Net Working Capital*</u>*.*

⇒ <u>**Solvency Ratios**</u> **(Long term Ratios):**

10) **Debt–equity Ratio (** <u>**Based on Total Debt–equity**</u> **)**

(A) Total Debt –equity Ratio $= \dfrac{Total\ debts}{Owner's\ Fund} \times \textbf{100}$

❖ *Total Debt = Long Term Liabilities + Current Liabilities*

❖ *Long Term Liabilities includes :-*

Debenture, public deposits/fixed deposit accepted, long term loan (secured loan ,unsecured loan, bank loan, mortgage loan)

❖ *Owner's fund = Equity share capital + Preference share capital + Reserve & surplus + Profit & Loss account (credit balance) – Fictitious assets – Profit & Loss account (debit balance)*

❖ *Fictitious assets includes :-*
preliminary expenses, debenture discount, share discount, underwriting commission, advertisement suspense account, expenditure not written off, profit & loss account (debit balance)

(B) Based on Long term Debt–equity

$$Long\ term\ Debt\ -equity\ Ratio = \frac{Long\ term\ debts}{Owner's\ Fund}\ x\ 100$$

Note : *When there is no specific instruction, calculation of Debt – equity Ratio is expected based on* **Total Debt – equity Ratio.**

11) *Total Assets to Debt Ratio* $= \dfrac{Total\ Real\ Assets}{Debt\ (Longterm\ Liabilities)}$

❖ *Total Real Assets = Total Assets – Fictitious Assets*

❖ *Total Real Assets = Fixed Assets + Investments + Current Assets*

12) *Total Proprietary Ratio* $= \dfrac{Owner's\ Fund}{Total\ Real\ Assets} \times \textbf{100}$

Proprietary Ratio (Based on Equity shareholders' Funds) =

$\dfrac{Equity\ shareholder's\ Fund}{Total\ Real\ Assets} \times \textbf{100}$

<u>*Note*</u> : *When there is no specific instruction, calculation of Proprietary Ratio is expected based on* **Total Proprietary Ratio.**

▢ PRACTICAL SECTION ▢

1. Calculate accounting ratios as asked.

1) *In the books of A Ltd. The sales at the end of an accounting year is **Rs.7,00,000** Cost of goods sold is **Rs.4,00,000** Calculate gross profit ratio.*

   *Form the books of **B Ltd.** It is Known that the rate of gross profit is **25 %** on cost of goods sold. Calculate gross profit ratio.*

2) *Gross profit at the end of a year as per books of C Ltd. Is **Rs.1,00,000**. Sales include cash sales of **Rs.3,00,000** and credit sales of **Rs.2,00,000** Calculate Gross profit ratio.*

3) *Cost of goods as per books of G Ltd. Is **Rs.8,00,000** Opening Stock is **Rs.2,00,000** and closing stock is **Rs.3,00,000** Calculate stock turnover rate.*

4) *Sales as per books of H Ltd. Is **Rs.12,50,000** Opening stock is **Rs.1,00,000** and closing stock is **Rs.3,00,000** Gross Profit is **Rs.2,50,000** Calculate stock turnover ratio.*

5) *Sales as per books of J ltd **Rs.12,50,000** Gross Profit is **20** % of Sales Opening Stock is **Rs. 1,00,000** less than the closing stock and average stock is **Rs.1,25,000** Calculate stock turnover ratio.*

6) *Debtors of N Ltd. Are of* **Rs.60,000** *and bills receivable are* **Rs.13,000** *Cash sales is* **Rs.1,35,000** *and credit sales is* **Rs. 3,65,000** *Calculate debtors ratio.*

7) *As per books of P Ltd. Debtors are* **Rs.30,000** *and bills receivable are* **Rs.2000** *If the total sale is* **Rs.3,65,000** *and* $4/5^{th}$ *of which are credit sales, Calculate debtors ratio.*

8) *The Following balances have been taken from the books of Q Ltd.*

Particulars	Rs
Debtors	1,00,000
Creditors	3,00,000
Credit balances of Bills account	50,000
Debit Balances of Bills account	1,00,000
Purchases	15,00,000
Sales	30,00,000
Working days in the year	300

All Purchases and sales are on credit Calculate debtors ratio and creditors ratio.

9) In books of R Ltd. Creditors are **Rs 1,26,000** Credit purchases during the year are **Rs.7,30,000** Calculate creditors ratio.

10) Creditors and Bills payable as per books of T Ltd. Were **Rs.42,500** and **Rs. 5000** respectively. Credit purchases during the year amounted to **Rs.3,75,000** Working days in the year are **300** Calculate creditors ratio.

11) Books of W Ltd. Shows the following particulars at the end of the year Net profit **Rs.1,79,000** before deducting debentures interest of **Rs.30,000** and taxes **Rs.74,500** Total sales during the year **Rs.2,98,000** Calculate the net profit ratio.

12) P & L Account of X Ltd for the year ended **31-3-2002** is as under Total sales during the **year is Rs.11,60,000** Calculate the net profit ratio :

Particulars	Rs	Particulars	Rs
Administrative Expenses	70,000	Gross Profit	3,00,000
Selling- distribution expenses	55,000	Profit on sale of Furniture	10,000

Financial Exp (Interest)	30,000		
Loss by Fire	5,000		
Net Profit	1,50,000		
	3,10,000		3,10,000

(14) The following balances are taken from the books of **Y Ltd.** At the end of the year Calculate Net Profit Ratio from the given information :

	Rs.
Gross Profit	**1,35,000**
Cost of Goods sold	**2,02,500**
Net Profit subject to 50 % tax	**67,500**

(15) Some balances of **Z Ltd.** As on **31-3-2003** are as under:

Particulars	**Rs.**
B.O.D	**50,000**
Debtors	**3,50,000**
Bills receivable	**30,0000**
Workmen's Profit sharing fund	**40,000**

Creditors	1,10,000
Worker's saving accounts	30,000
Bills Payable	50,000
Outstanding Exp	20,000
Cash	20,000

Calculate current ratio and liquid ratio from the above information.

(16) Some of the balances as at **31-3-2004** taken from the books of a company are as follows From these balances calculate working capital turnover based on net working capital

Current assets	6,00,000
Current liabilities	1,50,000
Sales	22,50,000

(17) **The following information is available from the P & L account of a company.**

Particulars	Rs.
Sales	6,60,000
Gross profit	1,60,000
Operating expenses	61,000
Net profit as per Profit and loss account	99,000

Calculate operating ratio.

[78]

(18) *The following information is available from the books of a company.*

Particulars	Rs.
Sales	7,30,000
Gross profit	1,46,000
Administrative Exp	60,000
Selling and Distribution exp	22,000
Depreciation	27,500
Financial Exp (Interest)	10,000
Provision for taxation	13,250
Net Profit after provision for tax	13,250

Calculate Net Profit Ratio.

2. Calculate ratio as asked :

1) *Trading Account of D Ltd. Shows opening stock purchases and closing stock as* **Rs. 50,000, Rs.4,70,000, Rs.1,20,000** *respectively If total sale are* **Rs. 5,00,000** *calculate Gross Profit ratio.*

2) *Cost of goods as per trading account of E Ltd is* **Rs.3,90,000** *sales are* **Rs. 5,00,000** *Opening Stock and Closing stock were* **Rs.50,000** *and* **Rs.1,20,000** *respectively. Calculate Gross profit ratio.*

3) *Following balances are available from books of F Ltd at the end of accounting year.*

Particulars	Rs.
Opening Stock	50,000
Purchases	4,00,000
Carriage outward	5,000
Freight and octroi (**On Purchase**)	20,000
Freight inward	35,000
Closing Stock	120000
Cash sales	1,00,000

Cash sales is $1/5^{th}$ of total sales.

Calculate Gross Profit ratio.

4) *As per trading account I Ltd. Opening stock is* **Rs. 1,30,000** *Closing stock is* **Rs.90,000** *Purchases during the year is* **Rs.10,35,000** *and expenses relating to purchases are of* **Rs.25,000** *Calculate stock turnover or stock turnover ratio.*

5) *Information about L Ltd. Shows cash sales* **Rs.6,00,000** *Credit sales* **Rs.6,00,000** *rate of gross profit on sale 10 % gross profit on credit sales* **Rs.1,40,000.**

If Opening stock is **Rs.2,00,000** *and closing stock is* **Rs.3,00,000** *calculate stock turnover.*

6) Sales as per books of L ltd are **Rs.10,00,000** Closing stock is **Rs.2,00,000** Calculate stock turnover.

7) Debtors as per books of M ltd. are **Rs. 2,19,000** Credit sales during the year amounted to **Rs.10,95,000.** Calculate debtors ratio.

8) Books of O Ltd. Show debtors of **Rs.1,00,000** and bills receivable of **Rs.20,000** Total sakes is **Rs. 8,03,000.** Proportion of cash and credit sale is **1 : 10** calculate debtors ratio

9) Creditors are **Rs.23,500** and bills payable are **Rs. 6500** as per books of S Ltd. Cash sales and credit sale amounted to **Rs. 67,500** and **Rs. 1,82,500** respectively calculate creditors ratio.

10)   From the following information relating to U Ltd for the year ended on **31-3-2004** determine average payment period (Creditors Ratio)

Particulars	Rs.
Total purchases	1,00,000
Cash purchases	15,000
Credit purchase return	12,000
Balance in creditors account on **31-3- 2004**	9000

Balance in bills payable account on **31-3-2004   4000**

11)   **Certain balances as per balance sheet of V Ltd. Were as under :**

Particulars	Rs.
Creditors	**12,000**
Bills payable	**5920**
Bills receivable	**5000**

If cash purchases during the year is **Rs.24,000 (Which is 1/5th of total purchases)** *calculate creditors ratio* **(Take 300 working days in a year.)**

12)   *Total of administrative expenses selling- distribution expenses and financial expenses as* **per** *P & L account of a company is* **Rs.1,50,000** *and loss on sale of building is* **Rs. 10,000** *Net profit given after deducting these expenses and loss is* **Rs. 80,000.**

If sales are **Rs.11,25,000** *calculate Net profit ratio.*

13)   *Following balances are taken from Balances sheet of a company.*

Particulars	Rs.
Equity share capital	**5,00,000**
Fixed asset	**6,80,000**

Reserve and surplus	60,000
Current asset	2,20,000
Fictitious asset	20,000

Calculate proprietary ratio.

3. Balance sheet of PQR Ltd. As on **31-3-2004** is as under :

Liabilities	Rs.	Assets	Rs.
Equity Share Capital	4,00,000	Fixed Asset	3,38,000
Reserve and Surplus	2,05,000	Investments	2,04,500
15 % Debentures	2,00,000	Stock	1,55,000
Creditors	1,25,000	Debtors	1,32,000
Bills Payable	70,000	Prepaid Exp	13,000
		Bills Receivable	68,000
		Cash and bank balance	84,500
		Preliminary Exp	5,000
	10,00,000		10,00,000

Additional Information :

Particulars	Rs.
Total Sales (Cash sales are 1/4th of credit sales	7,50,000
Gross Profit	1,87,500
Net Profit (Before deducting debenture interest of Rs.30,000 and Provision for tax of Rs.1,20,000)	2,70,000
Opening Stock as on 1-4-2003	70,000

❖ **From the above information calculate following ratio :**

A. Gross Profit ratio

B. Net Profit Ratio

C. Stock Turnover

D. Proprietary ratio

E. Debtors Ratio (Take 365 days in a year)

F. Debt- equity Ratio.

4. From the following information relating to YM Ltd. For the year ended on 31-3-2002 determine average payment period (Creditors Ratio):

Particulars	Rs.
Total Purchases	8,40,000
Cash purchases	2,70,000
Credit Purchase return	30,000
Creditors as on *31-3-2002*	65,000
Bills payable as on *31-3-2002*	25,000
Working days	360

5. *From the following information relating to LMP Ltd. For the year ended on 31-3-2000 calculate average collection period (Debtors Ratio):*

Particulars	Rs.
Total Sales	18,80,000
Cash sales	5,40,000
Credit sales return	60,000
Debtors as on *31-3-2000*	1,20,000
Bills receivable as on *31-3-2000*	40,000
Provision for doubtful debts as on *31-3-2000*	5,000
Total creditors as on *31-3-2000*	20,000
Working days	360

…………×××××××××………

www.ingramcontent.com/pod-product-compliance
Lightning Source LLC
Chambersburg PA
CBHW080831180526
45168CB00006B/2643